To Mum with Love

LITTLE TIGER GIFT
An imprint of LITTLE TIGER PRESS
1 The Coda Centre, 189 Munster Road, London SW6 6AW
www.littletigerpress.com

First published in Great Britain 2013

Text by Josephine Collins, copyright © Little Tiger Press 2013
Illustrations copyright © Jill Latter 2013
Jill Latter has asserted her right to be identified as the illustrator
of this work under the Copyright, Designs and Patents Act, 1988

A CIP catalogue record for this book is available from the British Library

All rights reserved • ISBN 978-1-84895-519-6

Printed in China • LTP/1800/0507/1012

10 9 8 7 6 5 4 3 2 1

TO *Mum* WITH *Love*

I *love* the FUN we have together!

I *love* the quiet times we share...

a *good* book,

a cup of *tea* and

my **MUM** sitting next to *me*.

A chat with you *always* makes it better...

A smile from you *always* makes it better...

A HUG with you *always* makes it better!

For ALWAYS cheering me on...

thank you, Mum.

For *helping* me learn,

for the dressing up, and make-believe,

for bringing MAGIC to each day...

thank you, Mum.

Even when you make me want to

SHOUT...

I love you, Mum.

You *always* tell me I'm beautiful…

You *always* ask how my day has been…

I can tell you anything, and you *always* listen.

In ALL ways you're *wonderful*, Mum.

together at girly films.

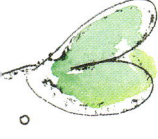

You're the *best* cook I know,

the *best* mender of things,

the *best* finder,

creator and organiser

of EVERYTHING.

Mum, you're the *best*.

For letting me go out and *reach* for the STARS –
thank you, Mum!

I don't always get it right…

but you're ALWAYS there for *me*.

For getting home *late*,

for making a MESS,

for not always listening,

I'm *sorry*, Mum.

Thank you for telling me I *can* do ANYTHING.

I feel so *happy* when my phone rings

and I see it's YOU.

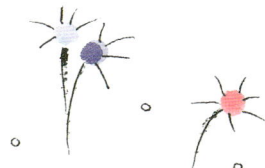

I *love* it when we sing along LOUDLY to all our *favourite* songs!

When you're not close,

my LOVELY mum,

I miss you!

For EVERY...

wrap up warm,

don't you worry,

goodnight, sleep tight,

well done, my darling,

thank you, Mum.

I don't tell you often enough

how *beautiful* you are and how *loved* you are...

my AMAZING, *wonderful* mum!